Find Your Flow: How to Get Wisdom and Knowledge from God

Dan Desmarques

Published by 22 Lions Bookstore, 2019.

Copyright Page

Find Your Flow: How to Get Wisdom and Knowledge from God By Dan Desmarques

Copyright © Dan Desmarques, 2019 (1st Ed.). All Rights Reserved.

Published by 22 Lions Bookstore and Publishing House

About the Publisher

About the 22 Lions Bookstore:

www.22Lions.com

Facebook.com/22Lions

Twitter.com/22lionsbookshop

Instagram.com/22lionsbookshop

Pinterest.com/22lionsbookshop

Introduction

Intelligence, as a set of cognitive skills, as conceived for social success, means nothing in the order of the universe. True intelligence is that which comes in the form of wisdom. And wisdom is the path of consciousness to the knowledge of oneself. Along such line of thought, this book seeks to describe how this kind of supernatural wisdom can be acquired by anyone.

How Does Mental Potential Develop?

Intelligence can be more rapidly developed if it is directed towards wisdom, being, therefore, a practical intelligence and associated to the happiness of the being, acquired by the awareness of his existential purpose. Whenever we find ourselves motivated on a given path, we learn faster. On the other hand, the mental connections that form when the neurons are energized by emotions, are much more complex, thus allowing an acceleration of what we consider to be effective thinking. This effectiveness arises precisely from pragmatism.

Pragmatism is only relevant when reinforced by personal ambitions. That is why the way to the moral and social development of a human being can't deny his ego. When the being operates on his material universe in the sense of understanding it and thus becoming more aware of his relation to it, can more easily discover what is pleasurable and also be successful in it. For in what gives us more pleasure, we will find our personal interests and an opportunity to reform psychologically and spiritually.

In this state, we can evolve more rapidly also towards the discovery of the reason for our existence, the so-called existential purpose. In this walk, logic will assume a proportion equal to the level of happiness felt by being on the right path, which will then produce a higher energy that will boost us towards progress. Whenever we are reinforced, excited by an activity that has a deep meaning for us, we also feel more capable, as opposed to the engaging in activities that we do not like and that discourage us. And it is a fact that the vast majority of people age faster by performing functions they detest. When we choose a job we do not like, what we are really doing is exchanging our time, our vitality and our health, for money. We are more amenable to physical illnesses, mental wear, depression and major accidents in these situations.

The Relation of Happiness with Vitality

We can say that understanding generates happiness and happiness generates energy, energy creates motivation and this drives the movement of spiritual development. In this cycle of endless learning, a being becomes transformed and, in this permanent change in interaction with the physical universe, he acquires greater potential for survival. In this potential, he finds the development of his intelligence in action, which is better known as wisdom, because it refers to the learning developed by the experience of living, namely, in feeling the effects of personal actions.

When the way is right, the being can develop with greater certainties about his personal identity and spiritual journey. In this journey the person may rise mentally to a level where the potentiality to act on matter is greater.

In other words, the more we transform the material world through action stimulated by pleasure, the more we transform ourselves in the process as well. And thus, the pleasure of living, the pleasure of working with an unselfish purpose, the purpose of feeding the ego with meaningful gain, all lead to a deep spiritual transformation that expands our level of consciousness and raises our intellectual potential, as any study in psychology has proven. It is at this point that all extrasensory abilities can arise, beginning with precognition and telepathy. And truly, people of high level of success in finances and social affairs often explain how they make decisions based on visions, dreams, or strong intuitions.

Success is never so much a fruit of individual potential as it is the fruit of a meaningful spiritual decision. We need to learn to believe in our potential even before we manifest the results that find explanations in this.

How Do You Gain Superhuman Powers?

At the top of the development of wisdom about the world, less common skills, such as extra-sensory powers, emerge. These powers, in their various levels of influence, scope and control, are the result of many stages of trial, pain, and perseverance. They are gifts to all beings who have persisted in self-development, beyond the challenges to which the material world has forced them.

Naturally, not all people acquire them, for the trials for some may lead them to the hell of existence. The difference lies in the awareness of the purpose of life, beyond the pain it includes. Therefore, "never assume that the obvious is true" (William Safire). It is not so much to say that the sufferer develops more spiritually, but rather that spiritual consciousness is directly dependent upon the action of the subject on himself, in the sense of understanding his physical universe and surpassing it, concentrating on his personal will, in acquiring his dreams.

Achieving more success and more wealth in life always includes a greater degree of responsibility, power and influence that must also be taken into account with equal importance.

All who can see the meaning of life beyond its physical materiality, or the pain it may assume in the course of existence, can more easily develop the wisdom necessary for understanding the existential purpose, and on the way to the vision that God has empowered them with, to understand about their identity, discovering all the paranormal potential they hold. And if we want to put this influence on a practical level, it is enough to think that the best way to help others is through monetary donations, which are more accessible to those who have gained wealth through success in their lives.

The body is limited, but the spirit possesses a potential that goes far beyond matter, that is, making use of the body, which serves as a vehicle to consciousness.

How Do We Heal?

All diseases can be healed through the potential that resides in the spirit, because it holds the projected power for life in the being. However, it is consciousness, which resides in the soul, that defines the evolution of the individual's life. In other words, by the consciousness one lives or dies. In our consciousness all answers to the dilemmas and problems of existence can be found. And since consciousness controls the nerve centers of the body and the main glands, affecting the immune system, we can even say that consciousness is directly related to the expansion of the life of a human being.

Illnesses arise and regress at the same point — the body, through which the consciousness of the spirit manifests itself. Therefore, only a sick spirit would develop a sick body. But if the spirit is in itself perfect, we can say that only the soul that does not find itself living in the consciousness of itself can direct the body to sickness and death.

"Being human, we can only receive infinite truth in finite doses" (Norman Grubb). When discussing the soul's potential to free us from the tentacles of pain, it is also important to analyze our ability to become aware of our potential to be happy and change habits.

In thousands of scientifically proven cases of cancer regression it was found that patients had several points in common, all related to the ability to make mental changes, to be happier and responsible for the future; and food, by focusing on natural foods such as vegetables and fruits.

It is in the final balance between the capacity to be happy and the inability to face the existential dilemmas, that the soul finds a way to balance itself in the control of the energy that governs its physical body and the material universe, being that all the diseases interact in this dynamic, usually composed of numerous sub-dynamics. Such sub-dynamics, though fully encompassed by the subconscious plane, assume only the force we allow them at the conscious level. Therefore one can say that the degree of consciousness of an individual is proportional to his level of unconsciousness.

The key to the resolution of all illnesses lies then in the principles of existence and the creative and dynamic force of the Universe as being one and the same. It is in the laws of God that one finds the DNA of life and death, and the secret of the mechanism that governs both. When we study the chemistry of the body, we are merely observing the manifestations of that force. It is in the relationship between spirit, mind, and body that we understand the laws governing that force.

The Relationship Between Happiness and Health

Considering that God wants humans to be happy, in the development of happiness we find the power to revert diseases to the original state of health. Exploring our individual consciousness, we also learn about the mechanism that governs our identity and spiritual path. In this consciousness lies the key to harmony, in health and satisfaction.

These principles are valid for all that energy associates, for the rules of the cosmos unite all material and immaterial. Matter has as much power over the spirit as it abdicates to control matter. That is why it is said that we must pay attention to the road when we drive. If we pay attention to life in the same way, we make fewer mistakes and subject ourselves to less unforeseen events. In this growing association of positivism, we can eliminate the negative.

On the other hand, we can't control the negative flow with the acceptance of its manifestations, namely, focusing our attention on diseases and problems. For by focusing on the negative flow, it creates associations with this negativity, which causes us to waste time, which could be applied to something positive, to feed a positive state.

For example, when we focus on treating a disease, we can't occupy our mind all the time with worry about disease. On the contrary, we must deal with the solution, creating health by strengthening our immune system.

Foods and thoughts that promote health are always more desirable than drugs that only try to maintain it, and that end up in this process by postponing only the course or modifying the way of acting, creating the illusion that it was prevented, while the truth is that the opportunity given to the body to combat has led to the positive result. It is a result obtained indirectly by the use of the drug, but can be obtained directly by the thought and through a diet that promotes physical energy and health.

Although it is difficult for most people, and even scientists, to compare the relationship between a person's physical state and his mental state, this relationship becomes progressively more evident over time. A person with aggressive tendencies, for example, may develop psychopathy. That is, through the adrenaline need of aggressiveness, initiates risk behaviors, namely, sexual risk behaviors, promiscuity, etc. He or she may then start using drugs in the pursuit of more pleasure. And all this leads to a lack of control that is translated at the hormonal level. Hormones, on the other hand, can affect the immune system, which then leads, due to immune deficiency, to the appearance of cysts, cancer and other diseases. And that's how a person ends up dying young.

It is believed that between 70% and 98% of diseases are psychosomatic. And this can be proven by the way people respond to cures. Some people survive with certain surgeries and others die, regardless. But we can observe how this process is gradual, over many years, and with very similar symptoms, emotional and psychological. As absurd as it may seem, this leads us easily to conclude that some values, such as discipline, self-control, and serenity, kindness, and empathy, lead to a more enduring life.

How Can Mental Illnesses Be Cured and Behavior Changed?

Psychological illnesses in general can be solved by helping an individual act on his own world by developing a potential to be happy and to know himself. By helping someone in accomplishing what makes him happy, we can increase the quality of his thinking. This because the determination and concentration aided by positive emotion exponentially increase the number of synapses in the brain towards a new behavioral pattern. And if we want to reform behavior, changing habits, actions and thoughts, this is the fastest way to do it.

A happy being has clearer and more objective thoughts. And, a more conscious being has more intelligent thoughts. Therefore, we know that mental illness can be solved by teaching about the purposes of existence that lead to the same result. For, the more one knows them, the more one can move in the direction of being efficient in life.

The difficulty in changing the behavior arises precisely from what one intends to change. That is, the strongest patterns of behavior and the most common thoughts create resistance to change, through mechanisms that control one's own decision-making capacity. That is why many people make stupid decisions in their life and against their survival. "A madman will deny more truth in half an hour than a sage can prove in seven years" (Coventry Patmore).

A person is confused only with his identity and the reality that encompasses him when losing the purpose of existence. He's like an adventurer lost in a virgin forest. On the other hand, we can't say that an intellectualized person is wiser, for true wisdom consists in knowing when to strengthen the thought that leads to success, and at the same time being able to reform all thoughts and ideas that lead to failure. The vast majority of people do not have such intellectual ability because they are not accustomed to thinking and do not know how to think effectively. And so, the ability to think is independent of the educational system and degrees of formal education.

Many in the field of psychology and psychiatry have attempted to explain such phenomena, like stupidity in intelligent people, by introducing terms such as "emotional intelligence" or "social intelligence," among others. But the truth is that any form of intelligence is only relevant when it comes to the processes and mechanics of thought and analyzed through them. It makes no sense, ever, to evaluate what can't be changed and corrected.

Ultimately, when the existential purpose is present, hope in life increases, because when we teach to achieve this purpose, life gains meaning and more easily can be found in the parameters that help to lead to a spiritual path. It is about teaching the individual to compare and learn to discern by comparison, so that, in resembling and differentiating, he can find the efficient and ideal attitude that allows him to be happy. The more happiness he can achieve, the more potential he has to live a meaningful life. For he who has lost himself in his mental disorders has lost the ability to distinguish between happiness and unhappiness, good and bad.

Hence it can be said that it is in the loss of the path of God, of supreme truth, that the insane live the hell of insanity. In the awareness of this way, all happiness and logic assume purpose. And evil, manifested in confusion, fear, and disease, progressively regresses according to the work done to reform thought connected with emotion. That is why art is the supreme therapy, capable of altering anyone.

How Can We Predict the Future Wisely?

Spiritual knowledge resides, to a greater or lesser extent, within all human beings. However, we can say that the more experienced spirits, which learn from their varied previous existences, will possess more spiritual knowledge, regardless of the age of their present body.

Spiritual knowledge can be more or less developed in relation to the action of a being in the reality that presents itself to him. Not always the awareness of spiritual knowledge is awakened, reason why many beings can only awaken in the interaction with the material world in which they find themselves. Knowledge of the future, increasing responsibility for the present material world, also increases the experience of consciousness in its journey through the acquisition of self-knowledge. Predicting the future can only give meaning to life because whoever sees everything, everything can, in the sense of being more capable and useful to divine will.

But, with greater knowledge and power comes an increase of responsibility. And, with responsibility, comes a greater need for action. Therefore, the beings who can see more will feel more pressure on their responsibilities. Seeing more implies the creation of linkages with greater dynamics in interaction in the present reality. As thought intensifies complexities at the level of mental synopsis, social utilitarianism increases the complexity of social action, and altruistic action in this way stimulates the potential to see more.

Wisdom is superior and unlimited because "Wisdom is found only in truth" (Johann Wolfgang von Goethe). Given our knowledge of more comprehensive dynamics, we are forced to interact with all of them to understand them better. In this depth of experience, we can achieve greater personal fulfillment, but we can also confuse ourselves in a world of appearances and similarities in which not everything that resembles mind or consciousness is real. Hence, increasing responsibility over what you can see also increases personal challenges along the way. We are not always ready for the truth.

On a personal level, I must say that the confrontation with the psychopathy of others has been to this day, my greatest difficulty, because it is difficult to accept that so many people have disgusting behaviors in their life. As much or more as verifying that ignorance is comprehensive and promoted by those who are made to represent themselves as group leaders. Or the fact that many people, the vast majority, spend a lifetime, eighty years or more, in complete darkness, without understanding the most fundamental values of life.

The life of those who see more may get more meaning, but it is not in itself, and for this reason, significant. The meaning of life lies in the awareness of the importance of life, which can only be achieved with responsibility for existence. The responsibility we hold over this existence must be formed, developed, perceived and understood, in interaction with others and with our desires. Whenever we can work to achieve desired dreams, we are giving ourselves opportunities to understand the meaning of our life. And whether we achieve them or not, we are becoming aware of the importance of existence and the relationship it has with the spiritual plane.

In short, with greater awareness of responsibility will arise a greater visualization and, with this potential, more can be perceived and assumed, or even accepted, leading the spirit to a greater understanding of itself. Existence is summed up in the making of permanent decisions that transform reality and consciousness into permanent interaction with the same reality.

How to Interpret Religious Wisdom?

In a world of human principles, no religion interpreted by them can be true as a whole, for consciousness is independent of moral principles, though it may find similarities in them. "The truth, as far as religion is concerned, is simply the opinion that survived" (Oscar Wilde).

Religion presents itself as a mere stimulus of the spiritual senses, and never as a true path or as food for the soul. It is necessary, therefore, for spirituality to break with the limitations of religious or literary dogmas, the works that govern the cults, in order to pierce the portal that opens among the successive cognitive traps, formed by human thought that the religion presents.

One can't say that there is a true religion, because, among truths camouflaged by philosophies interpreted by men, the lie becomes confusing. In all religions there is some truth, but only enough to hold the convict in a web of stunning and false sense of happiness. This is because happiness can never be outside of the being, but only in its direct action with the reality that interferes in his existence. The awareness that religion promotes may help in the attainment of happiness, but we can't affirm that a religious group, in itself, transmits happiness.

There are as many religions as possible arguments against the spiritual world, and because the argument starts from mental ability, it does not necessarily have spiritual correspondence. The minds of many can never validate the truth in the spirit of one. For, no being has full spirituality, but rather is in the way of its development. Therefore, none of his arguments may be true enough to be able to transpose a full truth into meanings. The only divine truth transposable to all souls resides in the spirit, waiting to be awakened by each one who possesses it, by direct action of the soul in its relation to the world and life itself. Only awareness in action allows us to see the truth, because the consciousness of one can't directly command the consciousness of another.

Although many religions have historically been presented as true, the human tendency to resist change has crystallized such groups into thought-forms that also resist change. And that is why even the most supreme religions tend to self-destruct.

The same goes for more intuitive religions. A communicated interpretation may give rise to a different interpretation, neither of which will be fully true; and, by mere interpretive errors, may deviate far from the divine plan of a full and happy existence. In this sense, it does not matter so much the interpretation that religion makes about the dichotomy of good and evil, or the way it interprets it, or even the side where it lies in this dichotomy, because the purpose of consciousness assumes a single path, independently of the starting point, and only one path allows for awareness.

It is normal for many adherents of seemingly beneficent and moralistic religions to commit harmful acts against themselves and their existence. This happens whenever religion is not enough to respond to the needs of the spirit. Consciousness will always need the means necessary for its development and will try to stimulate itself in the interaction with them, no matter how negative the behaviors may be. That is why the grave errors of the Catholic religion are counterbalanced by the depravity of many of its members through pedophilia and homosexuality.

In other more extreme cases, this was revealed in the suicide of hundreds of followers of alleged gurus. Many people are not aware of illusions until they are near death. And often, not even then.

For the lower consciences, perversity can often be the only means found to create some kind of meaning, albeit illusory; so that they may understand each other in the chaos caused by Ignorance. For the deceived mind, illusion is always meaningful, until the pain of being wrong proves otherwise, and it may take a lifetime, or never come to pass.

Many Satanists only regretted their mistakes shortly before they died. Others commit suicide, proving that repentance would never be possible without unbearable suffering.

Married with illusion until death separates them from the body, is how the lost spirits find themselves. That is why an attack on the lie is often perceived as an attack on self-love and fought as such.

How to Change Your Attitude

According to the work presented, it was possible to understand that the dynamics of existence obey a standardized set of which we are part and that is inserted in a divine logic. Thus everything that happens to us in the present arises from associations that respond to a set of spiritual premises in which we are the main co-creators of our reality. That is why true genius passes through an understanding of the sacred rules that dominate existence and abundance.

The "truth is beautiful, no doubt, but also the lies" (Ralph Waldo Emerson). However, everything begins and ends in the spirit, and in the study of these processes we find the reasons for the dilemmas of existence, but also the respective solutions.

Not only can we find an answer to physical and existential problems, but also to the attainment of happiness, in the purpose of existence and in the awareness of the meaning of life, namely, the purpose of ours. We thus know that the laws that make up existence are governed by a general plan that unites the whole universe. And it is in agreement with this divine plan that we find the reason for our existence and the happiness of existing. In fact, we find all the answers and solutions to the evils that arose from the absence of this. And this wisdom, which arises from a capacity to understand the invisible behind all visible things, is precisely what enables us to understand the relations between cause and effect in everything in our life, and also in the life of others.

About the Publisher

This book was published by the 22 Lions Bookstore.
   For more books like this visit www.22Lions.com.
   Join us on social media at:
   Fb.com/22Lions;
   Twitter.com/22lionsbookshop;
   Instagram.com/22lionsbookshop;
   Pinterest.com/22LionsBookshop.

www.ingramcontent.com/pod-product-compliance
Lightning Source LLC
Chambersburg PA
CBHW050451010526
44118CB00013B/1780